"HEREIN lie buried many things which if read with patience may show the strange meaning of being black"
(The Souls of black folk, W.E.B Dubois)

The Pan- Africanist Manifesto

The Pan- Africanist Manifesto:

A Prescription to the maladies that afflict the black race

Augustine J. Jeffrey

The Pan- Africanist Manifesto: A Prescription to the maladies that afflict the black race

First published in the anthology 'Building bridges: bridging the gap among African siblings' published by Achampong & Sons

Bible quotes: Good News Bible

Marcus Garvey excerpts: The philosophy & Opinions of Marcus Garvey, or Africa for the Africans, The Majority Press

LIBRARY OF CONGRESS CATALOGUING-IN-PUBLICATION DATA

Jeffrey J. Augustine, the pan – Africanist Manifesto: A Prescription to the maladies that afflict the black race

ISBN: 9798423203085
1. African studies 2. Pan Africanism
3. African philosophy   4.Black Studies

to all Pan-Africanists

Herein is written

Acknowledgement

It all started as a project for an anthology on how we could help bridge the gap among all African siblings from across the world. The soul of black people was first published in the anthology *Building bridges: Bridging the gaps among African siblings*. It has now expanded and developed into a book, and I am grateful to all those who were part of the anthology. From those who were present when the idea sparked in Baltimore, Maryland- namely: Albert Wagah, Czar Kijana and the publisher- Nana Achampong; to those who were part of the anthology- namely: Adjua Dubb in Washington D.C, Shantelle George in the Caribbean, and Nathan Edwards in England

Prelude

"The civilization of today has gone drunk and crazy with its power and by such it seeks through injustice, fraud and lies to crush the unfortunate.

But if I am apparently crushed by the system of influence and misdirected power, my cause shall rise again to plague the conscience of the corrupt. For this I am satisfied, and for you, I repeat, I am glad to suffer and even die…when Garvey dies a million other Garvey's will rise up…you can destroy the physical body, but you cannot destroy the souls of men, you cannot even destroy the mind of man. Again, I say cheer up, for better days are ahead. I shall write the history that will inspire the millions that are coming and leave the posterity of our enemies to reckon with the hosts for the deeds of their fathers…before Garvey goes, Garvey shall have laid a foundation for other Garvey's who will be more deadly in their sting than the one who passes off…Garvey hears the wail and cry, the cry of millions of our forebears crying from the grave- for what? I will not tell you; probably *another Garvey will tell you.*

…my work cannot be destroyed; my work will live through the ages… Look for me in the whirlwind or the storm, look for me all around you; for with God's grace, I shall come and bring with me countless millions of black slaves who have died in America and the West Indies, and the millions in Africa to aid you in the fight for liberty, freedom, and life.

…I am only the forerunner of an awakened Africa that shall never go back to sleep… if the enemy could only know that Marcus Garvey is but a John the Baptist in the wilderness." (Marcus Garvey, from the philosophies and opinions of Marcus Garvey)

(Marcus Moziah Garvey)
(1887-1940)

Part One

"...Egypt does everything wrong and staggers like a drunken man slipping on his own vomit. No one in Egypt, rich or poor, important or un-known can offer help" (Isaiah 19:11-15)

Chapter One

<u>It is Strange to Be Black</u>

Herein, lie unearthed many things- which if read with patience; show the strange meaning of being black.

Herein, lie unearthed many things which if read with patience; show how a race shall be redeemed.

It is a huge burden to belong to the black race, that if before birth, you were given a preview of your life as a black man or woman; and given the option to choose a race, you would probably pick another. The late King of pop music tried to change his race from black to white; then incongruously sang that *'it doesn't matter if you are black or white'*.

It is strange to be black in this world where the color **black** is associated with the negative. If your cat dies on a Tuesday, you can call that day the '**black**' Tuesday. The Tuesday of October 29, 1929, when the stock market crashed- at the onset of the great depression;

is known as *Black* Tuesday. The devil's color is **black**, you wear black during funerals, illegal trade is black market and predominant black neighborhoods in the U.S are well credited for crime!

Let us do ourselves a favor if we really want to lift ourselves up and begin by acknowledging that we are at the bottom of the human hierarchy. We are the most 'inferior' and most non-self-reliant race in the world. You must first acknowledge that you are sick before you can seek medical treatment, otherwise it would not be necessary to seek medical treatment if you were well. If the black race wants to stop other races from looking down upon it as inferior, the race must first acknowledge its 'inferiority'- otherwise there will be no driving force to make us strive to be perceived as equals – or better - by other races. If the black race wants to uplift itself up, it must first realize and accept that it is down.

Truth be told, there are more numerous, negative facts surrounding the black population more than any other collective race in the world. From the dreaded HIV AIDS, poverty, poor governance - be it in Africa or the Caribbean, crime, drugs and violence, rampant divorce, and single parenthood among and the African American community, wastage of the youth… and the list goes on.

These negative facts beg the question: could this be the reason why we of the mighty African race are called blacks? Are we black people, at home (in Africa) and abroad called blacks because of our skin complexion, or is it due to the negativity we bare as a race?

When sins are washed away, we are told people become as white as snow. White is holy color, angels' glow in white – and white is also the bride's dress. Incidentally, white is what we call members of the 'superior' race in the world.

If we are called blacks due to our complexion, due to our skin color which is commonly dark, - then why are members of the white race called white when their complexion is not white? Members of the white race do not have white skin. That is not white, and it is not right to refer to them as whites. Are we that color blind that we easily accept that whites have white skin- and are therefore referred to as white people? Or did they call/ brand themselves the title of whites, as a symbol of the positivity they bare as a race, and the superiority they enjoy among the races of the world? Did they call/brand us the title blacks, as a symbol of the negativity we bare as a race and inferiority we enjoy among the races of the world?

Satan and God are two opposites, and one is holy while the other is evil. Holy and evil are two opposites. The colors black and white are two opposites; one is associated with holiness while the other with evil. Holy is positive, while evil is negative, and the black, white titles remain a mystery.

Extinction

According to the world, we as black people all over the world- have a dark future. We are of no great help to the world, safe for the economic prop we offer due to our blindness. If the world considers us to be of little help, then what would compel them to save us from destruction?

Our mighty race is credited with numerous problems: a leading beggar and bagger to the world, a parasite, a burden, and Africa relies on foreign financial aid and help for its own governance. We are always in need and soon we will realize that a friend in need is a friend to avoid.

The strange meaning of being black stretches as our Nile for you are also marked for death. We are subjects fit for mass extermination, even as the misguided Ugandan dictator Idi Amin dumped beggars into the source of the Nile for death, so shall we the black race be dumped into the ever-flowing river of death. Washed away into history books, as a race that once was, but one that never made it to the finish line in this race called life.

"…in another two or three hundred years when the stronger races will have developed themselves. They will not then as they have not in the past, allow a week and defenseless race to stand in their way, especially if in their doing so they endanger their happiness, their comfort and their pleasure." *(Philosophy and opinions of Marcus Garvey)*

In the above God given message to black people, Garvey also talked of how the weak aborigines were exterminated by the white invaders (the world manipulators) in Australia. They found a weak defenseless race in their way and got rid of them. He also talks about what happened to the weak North American Indian who was also exterminated by the white invaders- the world manipulators.

Since we seem to be a stumbling block, occupying vast wealth in terms of natural resources in Africa, we seem to be in the world manipulators' way, hindering their acquisition of vast wealth in Africa freely. We are endangering their happiness, their comfort and pleasure, and if this is the case- we are marked for death.

Ours is a race that is to face extinction if not saved in good time. Why is Africa the worst hit by the AIDS pandemic? Why do we have three quarter of the world's HIV-AIDS cases in sub-Saharan Africa? Was AIDS created by the world manipulators to exterminate us? "Hell no!" they cry out. Then why are African Americans the worst hit by the AIDS pandemic in America? Is this a biological weapon of mass extermination?

Marcus Garvey taught that:

"The Negro now stands at the crossroads of human destiny. He is at the place where he must either step forward or backward. If he goes backward, he dies; if he goes forward, it will be with the hope of a greater life." *(Philosophy and opinions of Marcus Garvey)*

Our African race- the black race; is one that will be difficult to save but one that shall get saved. Just as Christ our Lord and savior, saved us from eternal death at Calvary- so shall he save us from this worldly eternal death, even as our forebear helped him carry his cross. He stretches forth his hand towards us, as we did, so that we the Africans can be the ones to save our race… for Christ already saved us and gave us the right to claim and live our freedom. We are the saviors of ourselves. And for this reason- we herein tread on through this treatise. It is a journey in pursuit of our salvation, and it will culminate the day our mighty race shall truly be emancipated. Emancipation shall bridge the gap we have within ourselves as a race, and between our race and the other races. Emancipation will strip us off 'the veil'.

The blueprint

Pieces of information is scattered all over, lying here- lying there in different forms. Right from the biblical days, we have had in our possession, the necessary knowledge required for our successful redemption.

It is true that God created everyone in his own image. We are all gods and he created all of us equal. No one was created superior to the other and what one man can do, another can do and sometimes even better! So why is the black race not doing as well as the other races when we are all gods on this earth?

Something or someone must be the problem. Someone or something must be the one hindering our prosperity and making us not live up to the expectations of God- which is for us to live happy, prosperous lives. Someone or something must be stopping us from doing what other races are doing and this is our enemy, and we must find and defeat this enemy.

We must also now acknowledge that it is true, and it is a fact- that there is a huge gap between the African race and other races of the world. It is sad but it is a fact- that there is a huge gap between the various African communities all over the world- from Africa to The Americas to Europe. What we must accept is that for the African Americans to fully develop, become self-reliant, and earn the respect they deserve; Africa must first fully develop, become self-reliant, and receive the respect it deserves.

For Africa to fully develop, become self-reliant, and earn the respect it deserves; African Americans must first fully develop, become self-reliant, and receive the respect they deserve. Blacks in the Caribbean and Europe must first develop, become self-reliant and earn the respect they deserve. No one segment will ever move ahead successfully by itself, otherwise why do you think African Americans still have the highest poverty rate in America, despite their being citizens of this blessed country in the world.

Napoleon Hill had this to say about America:

"In America you can achieve anything you desire in life; all you require to be successful in the United States is the desire to achieve success."

Why then, do we still have way more blacks in America languishing in poverty than the other races? Is it that they do not desire to achieve success? I think not, for even a lazy man desires success but may never achieve due to his laziness- he deprives himself of success by being lazy. The answer to our question is therefore that: No one segment of the African race will ever move ahead successfully by itself. We are united in strife and can only be free from strife if united, and that's exactly why African Americans remain poor on average, much as they are citizens of a country that *"you can achieve anything you desire in life."*

What we must accept is that for the African Americans to fully develop, become self-reliant, and earn the respect they deserve; Africa must first fully develop, become self-reliant, and receive the respect it deserves.

For Africa to fully develop, become self-reliant, and earn the respect it deserves; African Americans must first fully develop, become self-reliant, and receive the respect they deserve. Blacks in South America, the Caribbean and Europe must first develop, become self-reliant and earn the respect they deserve. No one segment will ever move ahead successfully by itself

This being the case, we have no choice but to bridge the gap we have as a race and unite as one strong African family just as we have a strong united Jewish family.

"The Africans were hypnotized then,

Even as they are hypnotized today,

Darkness they see,

Yet bright is their future.

As it was bright then

When their brains were darkened

They were brain washed then,

Even as they are brain washed today."

(Jeff Juma)

Chapter Two

<u>Are black people blinded by a veil?</u>

Standards were already set for black people and attributes were forced onto them to satisfy the world's needs. The world we are talking about here is a world controlled and 'perfectly' governed through the manipulation of the white supremacists – the world manipulators.

The whole world looks at us, not for who or what we really are- but for what the world manipulators said we are. The innocent world laughs and despises us as well. Our motherland we are told is the 'dark' Continent and our future is said to be 'dark'. But why is it so when our motherland is bathed in sunshine and our future as a race is prophesied in the bible to be bright?

Egyptians were black – Africans, during the biblical times. Inhabitants of ancient Egypt were blacks; and we are informed in the bible that *"Egypt will be a blessing to the entire world"* In this coming future.

We are far the richest continent on planet earth; we are blessed with immeasurable wealth and natural resources, but we never seem to see this wealth.

The Africans are naturally wise and highly creative. We The wise men of ancient Egypt have left a blueprint for the world to follow, we, builders of the pyramids.

"Go to hell Sir Jeff, why can't these Africans you praise so much build pyramids today? Why can't we see them excel in science and technology, not even in the inventions of any kind?" I can hear you ask in disgust. "It is the veil," I tell you!

We are unable to see our true God given abilities, same way we cannot see our God given wealth which is always stolen and transported out of our motherland. We are unable to see our wealth in the same way that we are unable to see that all black people are Africans whether you are an African American or are from Europe. Maybe we should have been called the 'blind race,' a people with a 'blind' future, and a 'blind' continent.

Do you know that the ancient Wise Egyptians we just praised were equally blind at some point in life? They allowed the Greeks to access their secrets and wisdom not realizing that they were giving them access to a 'Gold' mine. They gave them maximum access to everything and anything, and they were too 'blind' that they did not even see the visitors pack their loots into the chariots. The Greeks in those days were a curious people in pursuit of nothing but knowledge and wisdom. The ancient Egyptians failed to see that they were giving away 'Gold', the Greeks were not blind; they therefore took and made good use of information that the 'blind' men of Africa were unable to see!

Did God pass this blindness to us as punishment for our past terrible behaviors when due to our rich wisdom, we tried to rival him and compete with him? We were the builders of the pyramids, the wisest men on earth, the birth of civilization. The Jews even sought refuge in our motherland when they had no food to eat while we bathed in plenty food. All these factors must have gotten us carried away and we turned disobedient to God thinking that we could live without him. It is a sense of pride that Egyptians were the first to believe in monotheism, but was it the only living God, creator of heaven and earth that they believed in? I think not. So how could we escape God's wrath? The soul of black people had to be disunited from its offspring to tame these people who were trying to rival God. When you are not in union with your soul, you are bound to be attacked by any spirit that come your way, and most of the times they are negative spirits. The soul of black people is enslaved by God and will be united to us its children, when we redeem it through our acts of repentance and charity.

"...I will stir up civil wars in Egypt and turn brother against brother, neighbor against neighbor. Rival cities will fight each other, and rival kings will struggle for power. I am going to frustrate the plans of the Egyptians and destroy their morale... I will hand the Egyptians over to a tyrant, to a cruel king" (Isaiah 19:2-4)

"...King of Egypt where are those clever advisers of yours...they were supposed to lead the nation, but they have misled it. The Lord has made them give confusing advice. As a result, Egypt does everything wrong and staggers like a drunken man slipping on his own vomit. No one in Egypt, rich or poor, important or un-known can offer help" (Isaiah 19:11-15)

If this is the case, then we need to organize sincere mourning for our past wrongs against God and plead for his mercy. We must immediately organize a sincere day or period of atonement for all black people. God is loving and merciful, if we seek him in sincerity and truth; he will hear us for even the bible says that:

"The Lord will punish the Egyptians but then he will heal them. They will turn to him, and he will hear their prayers and heal them."

(Isaiah 19:22)

You are hidden by the veil.

We are a blind bunch of people who can't even see that 'as long as you are a black man- you are an African' (But remember what Prophet Isaiah wrote: *"...I will stir up civil wars in Egypt and turn brother against brother, neighbor against neighbor"* no wonder we sold each other as slaves, we helped the colonial masters in Africa, civil and tribal wars are never ending in Africa and we betray those fighting for our race everyday)

Our blindness is vast, and we do not see many things. This has over the centuries, or even millennia, created a huge gap within us as black people- and between us and other races. This gap was created in veil, is promoted by the veil, and will only be bridged in veil.

It is the veil. Our identity is covered by a veil, we are a people covered in veil, living under the veil, forced to wear veils.

The innocent world laughs and despises us because what they see in us, the traits they see in us- is what the veil we wear depicts. The veil thrown onto us by the world, by the world manipulators- has separated us from one another as black people across the globe and from other races as well; making us look and act inferior among other races. I will never forget the truth in the song:

 "Money- power- respect!

First you get the money,

then you become powerful,

and then gain respect."

Economical sustainability is the money for a race or nation. You must first become economically stable and self-reliant, and then power and respect will follow. Africa is the poorest continent in the world, much as we noted the fact that it is the wealthiest. Africa is poor through the veil and rich out of the veil.

The gap in wealth between Africa and other continents in the world; was created by the veil. Stepping out of the veil, you see wealth that if used diligently by the Africans, will make the motherland the world's largest economy.

We never see the wealth Africa is full of because our land never escaped the covering either. African land is also covered by the veil, and we only see what the veil was designed to show us but not the true Africa- not the wealth. We do not see the true Africa and its potential.

The veil shows poverty, suffering, HIV AIDS, starvation, pathetic governance, wars, works of charity-whereby we are a bunch of beggars and the likes.

How can other races see our goodness and treat us as equal men, when we ourselves as a race- are unable to see our goodness and treat each other as equals. We treat ourselves according to what the manipulators designed the veil to show us.

A special kind of veil was also put on members of other races, making them appear to us- different and superior than we are; as though we are not all of the same being- equally created by the same loving almighty father in heaven. We only see superiority in other races and lots of inferiority within the various groupings of our race.

We are disunited as a race because of the veil. We do not see ourselves as one family the way other races do. We are ready to kill one another, unable to see that we are killing our own family members. From the gang deaths in America to the tribal/ethnic deaths in Africa- we do not realize that the veil was made to make us do this. We do not know who we are. The veil makes us see each other as the aggressors to our numerous problems, hence we love to attack and hate one another. The veil has turned us into a weak race and as Garvey wrote:

"The difference between the strong and weak races is that the strong races seem to know themselves."

(Philosophy and opinions of Marcus Garvey pg. 91)

For surely an African American who claims that he is not an African, does not know himself. Don't you realize that the prefix 'African' in the African American titles you carry- means that you are an African melting in the American pot?

Indigenous Americans were a weak race and were exterminated by the world manipulators who formed America. America then became a community made up of immigrants, and you the African American came from Africa, but the veil makes you call a brother from the continent- "you African!" as though it was an insult and as though you are white. You are also an African, and the sooner we realize and accept this, the sooner we will rid ourselves off the nasty veil. To the white man's eye – as long as you are a black man, you are an African, a black bastard, a nigger.

It is different and strange to be black. But I am black, and if Garvey was a proud black man, then I am also proud to be black and even the bible says that *"Ethiopia shall stretch forth her hand,"* for God has welcomed us already- because he sees beyond the veil. It is an African, and no one else, who stretched forth his hand to help Christ

Jesus carry his cross on the way to Calvary. I am proud to be black, yes, I am black; black is my complexion, but black is not my future and black is not your future.

Simon of Cyrene helping our Lord out. Copyright 2008 New Melleray Abbey

"No matter where you come from, as long as you are a black man; you are an African" (Peter Tosh)

Chapter Three

<u>Black people or African people, who are we?</u>

A white American visiting Europe is still a white man. A white American in Europe is first a white man then an American. A European visiting America is still a white man. A European visiting America is first a white man then a European. The white settlers from Europe, who formed this great nation of America, did not cease to be whites when they came to America: they were and remain a united race.

On the other hand, an African American 'ceased' to be African and an African American visiting Africa is an American and not an African even though he is as black as the African from the continent. An African American will call the man from the continent with disdain - *"you African!"* - as though he is not one. W.E.B Du Bois in *The Souls of Black Folk,* wrote that:

"…an American, a Negro; two souls, two thoughts, two un-reconciled strivings; two warring ideals in one dark body"

The veil has made it difficult for the African American to realize that he is an African, despite the tag.

An African visiting America, living amongst African Americans is differentiated by the geographical adjective *'an African.'* Lucky for him, he is still an African – but this is only because the African American was told by the slave master, that his people (from the continent) - are a bunch unfit to be called humans. They are some 'animals,' in fact cannibals. Why do you think they show you wild animals on television when they talk about Africa in the white controlled media? This is to further instill into your minds that Africa is a continent inhabited by 'animals'. The African Americans hence disunite themselves from their kindred due to embarrassment. Who would like to be associated to man eaters? While in Helsinki recently, an ignorant but sincere European asked me if it was the first time/place I was seeing houses. She informed me that her parents told her that in Africa, people live on trees above the roaming lions below.

African Americans are embarrassed to be associated with Africa and its people; a veil was put on the African people from the continent making them appear different in race to the African American's eye. African Americans fail to see that before they become Americans, they are Africans; same way Jews in America will forever enjoy kosher food and be Jews, and then enjoy the honored status in the country.

But the African in Africa is neither immune nor safe from the veil. Before he is an African, he sees himself largely, first as a Christian or Muslim, and Francophile or Anglophile (depending on his recent colonial past)

 … *"a Negro; two souls, two thoughts, two un-reconciled strivings; two warring ideals in one dark body."*

Africans in Nigeria have killed each other due to religious differences, not realizing that they are first Nigerians before they divide themselves religiously. Their two major religions are foreign and were brought in by foreigners. How is it that they now identify themselves in accordance with their religious affiliations instead of their nationality? It is the veil! When we unite, we will be aware that we are first Africans – then we become Americans, Christians, or Muslims later.

"Christian-Muslim Mayhem in Nigeria Kills Dozens"
  (New York Times {www.nytimes.com}, January 19, 2010)

It is important that we declare at this stage of our race to salvation, that *"as long as you are a black man- you are an African,"* as the reggae legend Peter Tosh sang. An African American in the eyes of a white man anywhere in the world, is a nigger and an African in the eyes of a white man anywhere in the world is a nigger. United he is in his view of us, calling us by the same name while we call ourselves by different names; failing to see that we are one. The world manipulators know that we are one, yet they made us not to see ourselves as one. Divided we are, not seeing ourselves as one while we are covered in the different shades of this veil.

The mighty Reggae legend Peter Tosh

Of what race is the African American? Of what race is the African at home in Africa? Of what race is the African in South America, the Caribbean or Europe? Is there a race such as African American race, Africa race, Jamaican or Caribbean race? Or is it one African race? Division was part of the ploy by the white supremacists to confuse and disunite the freed slaves and to totally disunite the African race. *"Sitting at the table doesn't make you a diner, unless you eat some of what's on that plate. Being here in America does not make you an American. Being born here in America doesn't make you an American."* *(Malcom X)*

Why is it that the white population sees all black people as Africans irrespective of the country or continent we come from, and the white supremacists are determined to exterminate all of us irrespective of our geographical location? Is it because they know that "as long as you are a black man- you are an African"? In that case, would it not be wise for all black people all over the world to unite as a people who have been gathered by an enemy who intends to mass exterminate them?

Unity

Unity is strength. A people united can never be defeated. With this in mind, we shall confidently acknowledge that we the African people are dressed in veil, suffering in veil- because we are disunited. Our resistance towards mental slavery and the likes of the Trans-Atlantic slavery was weak due to our disunity.

Today we are still too weak in disunity to stand up strong and free ourselves from the shackles and chains of every form of slavery bestowed upon us. Slavery needs the kind of disunity we have for it to thrive and play around with us at its own free will, fooling us around at ease. Influencing our lives through disguises while it lives in veil making it impossible for us to recognize it for what it really is. The strange meaning of being black stretches for even slavery – the biggest black people problem today, is in a world where black people look at it (view slavery); not for what it really is, but for what it manipulates our minds to believe it is.

This is the veil we black people live under and is why we live concealed lives from one another- ashamed of whom we are; full of hatred for our own kindred, but plenty of fear and admiration for the white race.

Unity of race therefore is the key to our freedom. To successfully emancipate ourselves from the veil, we must first unite. Slavery is united by its machinery; they speak in one voice and are determined to exterminate in one accord. How can we survive their evil plans while divided? Were they aware of the fact that we could never resist and win while divided when they divided us? Who divided us- God or the world? Who is the world in this treatise? Who is the innocent world?

We must immediately emancipate ourselves from every kind of suffering for God never created us to be a suffering race, fit for the jails in America, the most attractive to the biological weapon AIDS disease, companions to poverty… and the list goes on. To this end, a free and united black mind that is revitalized and self-reliant is what we need to bridge the existing gaps between the various communities of our race worldwide. This is also what we need to bridge the gap between our mighty race and other races of the world.

*"If you know the enemy and know yourself, your victory will not stand
in doubt."*

(Sun Tzu, The Art of War)

Chapter Four

<u>Who is the black enemy?</u>

Sometimes it seems like the more we seek answers to certain problems in our lives the more we fail. These are the times when we get convinced that answers to our life-threatening problems cannot be found. The nature of the problems we face prints illusions on our minds and we think that we are required to engage our minds in some serious thinking and searching, searching only in faraway lands. You see, the illusions cover the truth and the answers - which are usually at our fingertips.

From Napoleon Hill, we are reminded that:
"Before you can master an enemy, you must know its name, its habits and where to attack it."

In this treatise we embark on a journey to do just that, and we must now remind ourselves who our enemy is. Yes, remind ourselves; for we already know- but as we've just said: we are still "thinking and searching, searching only in faraway lands".

Who is responsible for all the woes facing the 'black' race be it in Africa, to the African American or the Caribbean?

Marcus Garvey educated decades ago that **the Negro is his own enemy.** He discovered the enemy decades ago – yet we still search for the enemy and accuse the 'white' man. It is as though we do not believe that the Negro is his own enemy. So, is this the reason why we see each other as the aggressors, and we are forever fighting each other; pulling one another down? But how can we be our greatest enemy? Don't we love ourselves? The strange meaning of being black stretches like our Nile for we do not even love ourselves. But how can we love ourselves while dressed in veils that make us hate and destroy each other?

You are the enemy.

It is the Africans who gave away their fellow African brothers and sisters to the Arab slave abductions and massacres, into the Trans-Atlantic slave kidnappings and massacres, and other slave abductions.

It is the Africans who helped the white colonial powers to establish their colonial rule in Africa, enabling them to loot our vast wealth and enslave us mentally while at the same time physically and mentally enslaving those given away as slaves in the Americas and the world over.

African countries are faced with the worst forms of governance where selfishness is the governing machinery. It is not the white man practicing corruption, dictatorship, or poor leadership in Africa- it is the Africans themselves.

In America, 'black' people enjoy disproportionately high mortality due to poverty, drug and gang-related violence. Families are broken due to this, and the 'black' youth who are the future of the race die at early ages because of so-called 'black-on-black' violence (it is not white on black violence). Brothers in the U.S have become jail birds and families are broken through the prisons; 'black' women are left lonely and become single mothers after their spouses are removed from the society. A good number have had their souls crashed and are now turning to fellow females. Yes, lesbianism. The only way we can help our race is by stating the truth, much as we may not like it. Hiding the truth will forever place us hidden by the veil.

The white supremacist forces are behind the woes befalling all African people both at home and abroad, but it is the Africans who inflict the harm onto themselves.

If it is, as we prefer to say- that all our problems as a race; are to a great extent due to the white hatred towards us, then it is crucial that we acknowledge that all this is so because we cooperate with them and make it possible for them to do unto us all the evil they wish.
We are our worst enemies, and we know this to be true. It is interesting to note that *"oppressor and slave are co-operators in ignorance,"* as James Allen wrote in his *'as a man thinketh.'* Always remember this before you blame the white man for the woes facing the black race.

The oppressors of this mighty race of ours (the slave master and colonial masters) would never have succeeded if we were united and with one mind – one black mind, one 'nigger' mind. If we were united and had one mind, we would have loved one another, supported and protected each other- for we would be one and the same soul which we are anyway, though the parent soul of black people is enslaved by God.

The white supremacists enslaved us mentally, instilling in us negative attributes about ourselves and demoralizing our spirits. It is this mental slavery that has led to our disunity, lack of love for our race and motherland, low self-esteem and lack of belief in our capabilities and cause for the missing burning desire to prosper in life.

We were mentally enslaved through propaganda, and this led to the current gap that exists between our race and other races of the world, and between the various communities of our own race. There is the economic gap where black population will always be the poorest in any multi-racial society, social gap where the black population is perceived at the bottom in hierarchy.

What we need to do right now is to lay down ways of turning the enemy into a friend, a lover, and supporter. This is an enemy we cannot kill or rid ourselves of because we are the enemies, you are the enemy of the black race - we are our own enemies. Black people are the cause of all the problems facing the race from Africa through Europe, across the Americas, round and about the world over.

Beware of Covetous!
'Beware of covetous' was the sermon given by new paradigm advocate Rev. Gene C. Bradford of the Full Gospel Tabernacle Baptist Church in Baltimore one Sunday morning. Covetousness, he taught, is too dangerous, and we must distance ourselves from its different shades, same way you would from the plague. His sermon quickly stimulated my thoughts and writing of this part on the three plagues of greed, envy, and jealousy, which makes it difficult for the 'black' race to prosper.

Greed, envy, and jealousy have been the biggest barriers against 'black' liberation, barriers against the development of the 'black' race the world over. We began on a journey through this treatise, identifying and accusing various circumstances as the culprits and enemies of 'black' liberation, barriers to the 'black' man's development away from the inferior cesspool we find ourselves in. We now discover that greed, envy, and jealousy have ensured that our woes prevail for eternity.

"Booker Washington aptly described the race in one of his lectures by stating that we were like crabs in a barrel, that none would allow the other to climb over, but on any such attempt all would continue to pull back into the barrel the one crab that would make the effort to climb out" (Marcus Garvey: The Negroes greatest enemy)

Greed has ensured that corruption thrives in governments in Africa and the Caribbean, greed has forced African presidents to become dictators just to ensure that they keep filling their pockets with wealth. This plague lured brothers into selling their very brothers and sisters as slaves to the Europeans; just to ensure that they got wealth and power from the slave masters. The same vice makes black brothers kill one another in the streets, the more they get from the drug money-the more and more they want and are ready to kill for that.

Greed, envy, and jealousy are destroying the black race more than slavery and colonization could have if the two vices were still as active out of the veil today. Maybe Rodney should have also written *'how greed, envy and jealousy underdeveloped Africa'*- for it is the three vices that made it possible for *Europe to under develop Africa-* as was the title to his book. The three vices have led Africans to under develop themselves even as I write this discourse.

In most of Africa, leadership is the gateway to the acquisition and protection of wealth. Africans on a large scale become leaders in governments as a way of acquiring vast wealth and power to oppress those under them. Representing the people's wishes or developing the lives of the people they represent is usually secondary and may take place when they are under public pressure and scrutiny. African presidents are usually the richest in their respective countries, rich through public theft.

They scramble for and ensure that they acquire as much wealth as they can- and will cling on to power just to ensure their continued gaining of immense wealth while subjecting the people into hardship. They rule their people and not lead them. Why do you think Africa is still underdeveloped? We have rulers and not leaders to guide and lead the people to better lives as has been the case in the Asian countries that are now economically ahead of the African countries that were economically ahead of them some decades ago.

Envy and jealousy have forever given the civil rights movements and liberators a massive blow in our communities world-wide. Start a movement today and you should brace yourself to fight fellow siblings who will then gang up to destroy your dreams [simply because they did not initiate the idea]. We are always jealous of each other. A 'black' man will decline to lend a brother a hand simply because he does not want his neighbor to prosper thereby leaving him lagging.

The truth of the matter is that we cannot all do the same things to help our race; all you need to do is to do your best in your area of expertise and support your brothers and sisters in theirs. If you are an eloquent speaker and you see the rise of a gifted publicist in your community, do not fight him and put him down; support him. Work together and through that unity you will create a formidable force to uplift the entire race, a force that nothing will dare to stop.

"For the problem of the Twentieth Century is the problem of the color-line."
(W.E.B Dubois, The Souls of Black Folk)

Chapter Five

<u>Slavery then mental slavery</u>

Slavery is the biggest black people's problem all over the world for the problem of humanity has always been slavery. The problem of the twenty first century is the problem of slavery.

Open your mind and stop limiting your intelligence to the trans-Atlantic slavery or labor slaves. Slavery is dressed in veil, covered in veil. Slavery disguises itself through various forms and we frequently fail to notice that we are all slaves. It makes us over dwell on the Trans-Atlantic slavery and other forms of manpower slavery as the only ways through which it thrives.

You will hear black intellectuals and leaders cry out for reparations, reparations for slavery in the Americas, and for the colonial sins in Africa. That is a good cry but not as helpful as we may deceive ourselves to believe. The reparation we need from the world manipulators is freedom of the mind - 'anti-hypnosis'. We should demand compensation by asking for our minds to be freed once and for all. Our minds were the first to be enslaved before we were physically enslaved or colonized. It is the minds that were enslaved and colonized, not the people. Freeing only the people was freedom in veil. Freeing their minds was the freedom outside of the veil and was hidden from us by the veil. Therefore, we are not yet free men as we deceive ourselves to be.

Slavery is a natural force and is necessary for life to thrive. Adam and Eve became the first human slaves the moment they were created by God. The angels of God were the first slaves for God created them also as his servants. Angels according to St. Augustine – are the "mighty ones who do his (God's) word, hearkening to the voice of God's word," (ccc 329). They must do as God commands otherwise they become like Satan who was cast away from heaven into hell because, as an angel of God, he refused to do as God commanded. This being the case, are angels not slaves of God?

Adam and Eve were created slaves of God, created to do what the almighty creator wanted – what their master wanted them to do. "I am putting you in charge of the fish, the birds, and all the wild animals," (Genesis 1: 28).

God created man to take care of his creation here on earth; you are therefore God's 'slave,' his servant charged with the duty of taking care of his creation here on earth.

God commanded humans to "have many children" and fill the earth. He then made sex to be a powerful force of nature ensuring that man and woman crave for sex thereby procreating. You had to be made a slave of sex to guarantee that procreation takes place as God commanded – whether you like it or not.

Adam and Eve were slaves to God's will; they had to do as God wanted. They were slaves to God's rule that they were not to consume the fruit in the middle of the garden, and you know what happened when they disobeyed. Even as a slave is punished by the master for not obeying commands- even so was Adam and his wife Eve punished by God, their master.

God desired to achieve something when he created the universe, we are therefore slaves to this desire and even as slaves in the Americas got whips, so shall you be 'whipped' by God for not obeying him.

God knew that the fruit in the middle would make man a slave to sin and warned against it. Adam and Eve became slaves to sin when they listened to the devil, they became slaves to a slave; the first people to become slaves to a slave when they yielded to the devil's temptations. We now had two forms of slavery- which we could choose from; Godly slavery which is the noblest form of slavery, and it leads to eternal life, and a slave to sin and the devil which gives lots of short-lived pleasures to the flesh but plenty of sorrow to your soul- and leads to eternal death. Your soul will be in sorrow when you become a slave to evil ways of life because it knows exactly where it will end up at due to your evil ways. It is your soul to burn in hell for eternity, and not you the flesh. This is to say that you will be doing injustice to your soul when you allow the devil to enslave you now, then your soul burns for eternity in the afterlife.

The devil was a former angel, so he was also a slave like the other angels (slaves to God) before he formed his own class of slavery. As a slave to sin, evil and the devil; you are basically a slave to a slave;

and a slave to destruction for the devil leads to nothing but your destruction – oh what a shame! As a slave of God, you are a slave of the Almighty creator; a slave to the master and giver of eternal life, a slave to love- for God is love.

When asked by a teacher of the law what the greatest commandment was, Jesus replied that: *"love the Lord your God with all your heart, with all your soul, and with all your mind… love your neighbor as you love yourself,"* (Mathew 22:37-38). Christ then went ahead to make it extra clear that you are a slave to love when he said that *"the whole law of Moses and the teachings of the prophets depend on these two commandments."* (Mathew 22:40) You are enslaved to the two great commandments.

Life is all about slavery no matter who you are. A free man will do as he pleases, while a slave will do what pleases the master, what the master wants. By wanting you to serve him and for his will to be done on earth, God made you his slave-a slave to his will, *how can a pot question the potter?* Ever wondered why Christ taught us to pray that "Our father in heaven… *your will be done* on earth…"? You are a slave of the will of God. God had to create you a slave of his will for you to serve him, otherwise, as a free man; you would never have cared about him.

Slave the master

So, we can safely agree that life thrives best through slavery and its numerous forms. Slavery has over the millennia transformed itself, taking up various shapes and forms. Slavery is the momentum to life; slavery is what keeps life going. Slavery is what gas is to a car, it is your fuel. Mental slavery is the momentum to life; mental slavery is what keeps life going. Mental slavery is what God uses to bind us to his law. Slavery through its trickery and disguises is what makes you do things.

For anything in human life to occur, some form of slavery must occur. You would never even attempt to do any good in life if God never created you a slave to goodness and that is the reason why he created slavery. He did it out of love and he only uses it for love, unlike humans who use slavery in its various forms for selfish gains.

Slavery is master in your life. If you want to achieve anything in life, you must first become a slave to the thing you so desire. When you desire pleasure, you must become a slave to pleasure before you can have the pleasure you so desire.

You will have to do as pleasure dictates, pleasure will lead as you follow; only doing as it pleases. Pleasure will present to you opportunities that will lead to your satisfying the desire for pleasure. Pleasure will then force you to indulge in one or many of the opportunities, failure to which you will receive no pleasure.

At that moment, you will have become a slave who has to do as the slave master (pleasure) says.

"Drink!" pleasure will entice you through your mind, and you will drink because if you do not, you'll not have pleasure if drinking alcohol is one of your preferred forms of pleasure.

You must indulge in one or more pleasurable situations presented to you in your mind by pleasure your slave master- you are now in bondage! If this is the case, is it not correct to say that at that moment you are a slave whose mind is coerced into leading you to indulge in activities alluringly presented to it by the slave master called pleasure?

How about when you want to buy a house? You will need money to do that, and that is when you become a slave again. For you to acquire the amount of money you require for the purchase, or to ensure that you have enough for your mortgage; you must become a slave to money. Slavery is the momentum in life, slavery is a must for life to be in motion- it is the driving force for all human achievements.

"You badly need me, huh?" money asks you.

"You have to work in order for you to get me," money will command you. This is a command that you will have to follow; otherwise, you will earn no money for the purchase, same way Jesus taught that the *commandment of love* is the greatest, if you desire life, otherwise you'll not have the real life- but the life given in veil by the devil.

"Go start a business and earn extra cash, if you really want to buy yourself that dream house," Money will continue influencing your mind for this slavery talks to the mind for it knows that *"man is mind"* and *"mind is the master- power that molds and makes," (James Allen)*. Mind is the master, the power that molds and makes you.

"Go steal1" such negative influences shall also be delivered to your mind by the slave master called money.

You are now a slave to money, and you have to pick one or more of the options put before you. The moment you think of getting some money, it starts enticing you; corrupting your mind with various tactics which will help you acquire it. This slavery is a force of nature that exists to give you momentum into action.

Slavery as a force of nature is designed to corrupt your mind or to entice it with the intention of making your mind to lead you into doing a certain thing or acting in a certain manner. The tricky part is that the enticement may be negative or positive depending on your thoughts. When you encourage thoughts of theft to dominate your mind, you are harboring negative enticements. When you encourage thoughts of love or goodness to dominate your mind- you are harboring positive thoughts.

The slavery we need to worry about is not the transatlantic one and all its negative consequences. It was but a symbol of the real slavery affecting our lives. The real slavery is a force of nature, and we also use it against each other in its various forms and shapes.

We today enslave each other through numerous means and forms, for us to get what we want; you manipulate others in order for them to satisfy your needs. Through natural instincts, you first enslave a person's mind by instilling in it ideas that will lead the person into doing or behaving according to your needs and satisfaction. The act of persuasion is simply enslaving a person's mind to do what you say, so that by so doing- you get what you wanted from him.

God wanted you to be good, he therefore instilled Godly ideas in your mind- feeding you with plenty of morality, and he thus enslaved your mind that way. Why do you get guilty conscious when you perform ungodly acts? Why do you think your soul will be in sorrows when you become a slave to evil? God enslaved you to traits of love and goodness- for you to desire Godly traits. Why do people feel great when they help other people out? God instilled the idea in your mind that it is a great thing to do that, he made you feel important when you help a brother as one of the ways to ensure that you love your neighbor.

The United States of America wants the whole world to follow its ideals and continues to enslave the world's mind through propaganda via the mass media. Hollywood is purely a factory of world mental slavery, a propaganda medium where even Americans are made to think and act as was planned by the founders of this great nation. Americans are generally patriotic thanks to scenes coming from Hollywood where saviors of the country are crowned national heroes. Poor African nations never see such things in the media and have nothing to compel them to be patriots, but plenty to repel them. In Kenya, those who fought for the country's independence are among the poorest citizens, some are even unknown to the Kenyan public.

Man is mind, what is in a man's mind is what that man becomes. What the mind is made to accept and believe is what the man eventually comes to desire to be or do. Enslave a man's mind, instill in it through propaganda and persuasion what you want, and the man will give you what you want. Carefully crafted propaganda when instilled in a man's mind will surely give the required results for as long as there is no carefully crafted propaganda that disputes or corrects the motives.

Wars begin in the mind, and you first strategize in your own mind. You also must first kill the enemy's mind before the physical war starts. War cries are for the purpose of instilling confidence into the warriors' minds and scaring the opponents' minds. Once you defeat the opponent's mind, he will be too week and scared to put up any honorable fight against you.

"During the world war, much was heard about the effects of propaganda, and it seems not an exaggeration to say that disorganizing forces of propaganda were much more destructive than were all the guns and explosives" *(Napoleon Hill- law of success)*

Hollywood has made sure that America is mightier than all in the minds when it comes to military might. Right now, even a nation that may be mightier than America is inferior because its mind is made to believe so through the Hollywood movies and the American dominated and biased international news media like CNN.

Mental slavery is the biggest black people's problem today, even as it was when the Africans sold their brothers and sisters into captivity. Before brothers began giving away their fellow brothers and sisters away as slaves, they were mentally enslaved, and their minds were corrupted to make them perform such ills to the flesh of their own.

The great reggae legend Bob Marley, before his death; delivered and left us a strong message from the creator of our souls thus:

"Emancipate yourselves from mental slavery, none but ourselves can free our minds!"

Reggae Legend Bob Marley

Mental slavery is our biggest problem, and this is what we need to seriously investigate and deal with for our development, for our unity, for our bridging of the existing gaps within us as a race and between us and other races. Inferiority complex, lack of belief in self, Poverty, AIDS disease, corruption in governance, dictatorship, civil wars, gang and drugs indulgence, the alarming high rate of school dropouts among the African Americans are but results of the mental slavery. We must blame mental slavery more than we blame the Trans-Atlantic slavery or the colonization of Africa. Or maybe we should have used the wisdom and inspiration we gained from Walter Rodney for us to write *'how mental slavery underdeveloped Africa.'*

Reparation will never ensure that we never rely on compensation for us to develop and achieve social and economic stability; it will instead ensure that we forever rely on compensation. Reparation will encourage 'black' people to forever look for faults and wrongs done against them for them to receive some form of compensation. This will mean that we will keep blaming other people for our problems and try to receive compensation; we will have perfected the 'lazy' trend and the love for freebies.

If the colonization of Africa negatively affected the Africans at home, and has contributed vastly to their problems, and if slavery has negatively affected the African in the Americas, then 'black' people have been negatively affected equally by the same people. We should now stop blaming each other or accusing the other for selling the other or one for despising the other. Instead, we must understand that the enemy duped our minds and that's why we allowed them to use us to enrich themselves.

The Africans who sold their brothers did so because of the veil brought to the land by the slave masters. We now need to unite, remembering that *"none but ourselves can free our minds!"* Let us free our minds, for only then shall we be a united people, and gain social and economic prosperity. The rest of the world can be of help, but their help will only be commensurate with the efforts we put in helping ourselves. The 'developed' races can, and will be, of great help to us but their help can only be realized when we first free our minds and be the forces behind our own development; not them (the other races) forcing us to develop and showing us how. We are the creators and rulers of our destiny and James Allen reminds us that:

"A strong man cannot help a weaker unless that weaker is willing to be helped, and even then, the weak man must become strong of himself; he must, by his own efforts, develop the strength which he admires in another- none but himself can alter his condition!"

None but ourselves can free our minds. None can alter the black man's condition but the black man himself.

"If you don't stand for something, you will fall for anything"
(Malcom X)

Chapter Six

Blackipulation: The hypnosis of the black race

To 'blackipulate' is to manipulate the lives of black people across the world. It is to insinuate strange attributes to the lives, culture, affairs, and history of the black population.

Standards were set for black people, attributes forced onto them to satisfy the world's needs. The world we are talking about here is one controlled and perfectly governed through the manipulation of the white supremacists who are the world manipulators.

The whole world looks at us not for who or what we really are, but in accordance to what the world manipulators say we are. In accordance to the way they make us think and behave.

We look at ourselves not for what we really are but in accordance to what they say we are. Blackipulation is the act of crafting and preparing the veils and our wearing of the same.

Life is a race of the world's races, and every race is in pursuit of superiority amongst other races. We had the arms race before the previous world wars; today we have the race of the world's races leading to the current scientific and technological arms race - that is paving way to the impeding wars of the worlds. Every race and nations are in a struggle to become the world manipulators. The white race has been in control for the past 1000 years or so. Today the Arabs, the Indians, the Chinese all want a turn now. Are there signs out there that the African race is also preparing itself? Strangely, it is only the black race still in slumber and not much seems to be happening; it is as though the race does not really care. The other races and nations of the world are preparing for the supremacy war where only the fittest nations and races will survive, yet we slumber and are still divided and crab fighting.

Just as a thought, on whose side will the African American soldier be the day the supremacists decide to instigate war in Africa for the conquering and elimination of the Africans at home? Their biological weapon of eliminating black people – the disease AIDS is working well but not as per the anticipated speed. What might be their plan B?

If we are still divided now as we were when brothers sold their brothers into slavery, is it not likely that through the veil, the African American will be the foremost invader of Africa? Will not the supremacists use the veil to make him do injustice to his own family in Africa, before finally using him to do injustice to his fellow African Americans in America? Remember when slavery began, the Africans were lured into doing injustice to their brothers and sisters who they sold as slaves, and then later they were also used to do injustice to themselves by helping the colonial masters. Never forget that the supremacists never do the dirty jobs themselves, they will let you do it after they give you the veil that makes you act and see things their way - same way they did when we sold one another and helped them colonize us.

The races of the world, through the united efforts of their governments- are building military giants that are quickly threatening the white superpowers, while the African race and its nations are having their militaries built for them through foreign favors. While the former colonial powers help their former colonies in Africa build their military- by donating out -dated ammunition to the African military; they (former colonial masters) themselves equip their military with the new scientific and technologically advanced weapons that befit the impeding wars of the worlds. They meanwhile leave us in veil as we brag of our military might.

How will we survive the next world war and the war of the worlds which will all be wars of the races whereby only the fittest shall survive? The strangeness keeps widening for our extinction is impeding through wars if not through the biological weapons. We immediately need to unite and form a strong team that will defend us in these coming conflicts of the worlds.

Over the centuries systems have been set in place, systems are carefully set in place every day by different nations and races with a bid of becoming world's superpower. The first step has always been to enslave the minds of the people of the world to pave way for a race's superiority. Religious doctrines have been the most notoriously used and we know that the white invaders first introduced Christianity to the people before the invasion, and the Arabs also used Islam.

Christian missionaries were the first to enter Africa with their doctrine, paving way for the white colonial masters. By the time the colonial masters entered Africa, the missionaries had successfully prepared the Africans' minds leading to their warm welcoming of the colonial masters who later turned against the Africans- taking away their land and treating them with excess brutality that caught the missionaries unawares, sending them into shock and panic.

The Arabs used Islam as they came to satisfy their interests and to influence us in Africa. A huge number of Africans had their minds enslaved to the Arab's doctrine, and they had it rough when the whites came into the picture later. After the whites successfully took over from the Arabs in some parts of Africa, the Africans in those lands had their minds enslaved again. This time in accordance to the white man's doctrine which was different from the Arab's, this lead to massive confusion in the black man's mind- not knowing what to follow or what not to.

Usually, the success of this mental slavery and brain washing depends highly on the amount of crafted propaganda that will successfully be instilled in the victim's mind.

Luckily, there is always a barrier because the success also depends highly on the amount of crafted propaganda that had already been planted on the victim's mind before the attack. If the victim already had in his mind enough propaganda luring him to behave in a manner that protects his country or race- then the enemy is unlikely to have it smooth; and success will be minimal just as it was when the white supremacists tried to enslave the Arab's mind, and they have never succeeded with the Chinese either.

The white supremacists found the Arab's mind already in possession of positive crafted propaganda and this made it tough enslaving the Arab's mind as was the case in rest of Asia. It is only in Sub Saharan Africa where there was no philosophy of race taught to its people, and that is why the brain washing was a walk over. The whites and Arabs used their philosophy to instill inferiority into our minds and to make us believe and accept that we were created to be their servants and followers of their religion and ideals.

Incidentally, they both had their created religions, organized religious beliefs which had written doctrines. The white man's religious doctrine taught us that they were God's 'chosen people' as the God sent messengers. We read in the bible that the future of Christianity was to be with the gentiles for the Jews were to reject Christ. Christianity went to the gentiles in Rome and was spread all over and made dominant through the then superpower known as the Roman Empire. Christianity was promoted by the whites, is linked to them, they dictate what happens to the doctrine; and they 'own' it- while we are obedient followers just as they trained us to be -we see them as lucky and special people.

The Arab's religion of Islam talks of the Prophet Mohammed who happens to be an Arab, as the messenger of God, and he received the message of Allah. We now see them as lucky and special to have been chosen by God. We faithfully follow their doctrines without questioning and are ready to kill our brothers and sisters for the sake of the said doctrine. We do not even wonder why every race apart from ours has created its religion and teaches its people on the same.

It is emerging that various race used religion to instill positive propaganda into the minds of its people; Islam, Buddhism and Hinduism positively guide the minds of those it dwells, in vast areas of Asia.

It is now emerging that religion was used to enslave the Africans' minds and it is also emerging now that religion can be used to free our minds.

Christianity is twofold, church Christianity on one side and political Christianity on the other. The political wing always hijacks the good intentions of the church in a bid to conquer the world for the world manipulators. Islam is also two-fold, and its political wing does the same for the Arabs.

The political wings of these two world major religions were the most important aspects to the successful spread of the various doctrines and the conversion of people. This they did not for the love of God but for the sake of controlling the world. What we need to realize is that systems were set in place that by subscribing to the Christian faith, you are in essence adding the white supremacists points and making things head towards their ruling of the world as is planned. By subscribing to Islam, you are doing the same for the secret Arab rulers. From the beginning, each side needed recruits to help them in their mission and it was a race for the numbers.

Where is the religion that when you subscribe to, you will be adding to the black race? We are proud followers who would kill our brothers and sisters over foreign religions that serve foreign purposes. It has happened in Nigeria and how many times have we seen friends who all belong to the black race fight and insult each other over these two foreign religious believes? Why don't you put race first before religion? You are first an African before you become a Muslim or Christian; always remember that before fighting or killing your fellow African. When you kill a brother because of these foreign religions that marvel other races while belittling your race- you are in essence doing what the veil is designed to make you do.

"Armed with guns, machetes, torches, and bows and arrows, Christian and Muslim antagonists in central Nigeria's religiously volatile city of Jos have been fighting for three days in sporadic clashes that have left dozens dead, witnesses and local news accounts said Tuesday.

It was difficult to ascertain the precise toll in Jos, the scene of frequent religious violence over the past decade. Estimates ranged from 30 to 300 deaths, as the city was still consumed by mayhem Tuesday evening, with security forces descending on Jos in an attempt to contain it.

Gunshots could be heard throughout the city, and smoke from burning buildings was visible everywhere, witnesses said."

(The New York Times {www.nytimes.com}, January 19, 2010)

Know thyself.

"No man can be master of himself, who doesn't first understand himself" (Baltasar Gracian, The Art of Worldly wisdom)

When Africa came in contact with rest of the world, the Africans did not know themselves. No propaganda had been instilled into their minds telling them who they were, what they should do or can do. When the foreigners who had been taught about themselves came to Africa, they had it easy enslaving the minds of the clueless people they found in Africa. Remember Garvey taught that:

"The difference between the strong and weak races is that the strong races seem to know themselves."

"It is first principle that in order to improve yourself, you must first know yourself" (Baltasar Gracian, The Art of Worldly wisdom)

Why is it, that the other human races already had crafted propaganda instilled in their minds luring them to behave in ways that protect their race? Why are other races not as negatively enslaved mentally as we are? The answer is in our parent soul; our soul is locked up by God, and we need to reconnect with that. The soul of black people was enslaved by God, but it will be freed by him when we unite and be the saviors of the world in the coming wars of the worlds.

"Propaganda is the art of exercising power without possessing the means of power; it is the secret through which the powerless can overcome the powerful when they rest too securely in their strength."

(Eugen Hadamovsky)

Chapter Seven

Propaganda: The instrument of mental slavery

Propaganda is simply to instill into the minds of people ideas that will make them see things from your point of view as dictated in your propaganda. Propaganda can be positive or negative and is meant to make you think as desired by the propagandist. Aim of the propaganda is to make you act or do something or several things, in line with the thoughts instigated into your mind through the propaganda.

Unconsciously, man has always known that man becomes what man thinks he is, and what he thinks about all day. If you think that you are inferior, you will for a fact become inferior and it is impossible for a man to become superior when he holds thoughts of inferiority in his mind.

If you think that all you are worth in life is poverty, life as a beggar, a drug dealer, a jail- bird, an oppressed second-class citizen or the laughing bunch of humanity- then you are guaranteed to be just that, same way the day is guaranteed to follow the night.
Christianity is propaganda, and so is Islam and the education that you gain from schools. The propaganda of Christianity is intended to make you behave in a Christ like manner, following the teachings of Christ Jesus. Education at schools is supposed to make you do things as taught in the given course of study. Say for example you allow your mind to be fed on the propaganda of medicine, and you take the course and your studies seriously believing every single detail- you do know that that's how people become doctors! The propaganda of the study of medicine at the med school turned them into doctors, and the above are but only three good examples of the desirable traits gained from propaganda.

On the other hand, you may grow up while being fed with information that you are good for nothing and that your people are known to only excel in laziness, drug peddling, gang activities and different kinds of crime, sports and as entertainers. All around you, you see your people excelling in entertainment, gang activities, laziness and the other traits afore mentioned. You will thereby believe it to be true and harbor it in your mind that you are only good at those traits, thereby becoming one.

It is the propaganda that turned you into a drug dealer, a jailbird, a lazy man who cannot work to feed his family, an entertainer who further enriches the white controlled entertainment industry, or a sportsman making huge profits for the white controlled sports and advertising industry. You were not created only good at music or sports but since human beings become only what they think they are, or what they think about- you became the singer and not a lawyer who is a singer, because you thought that you were only meant to be a singer. It does not matter whether the thoughts were voluntary or were instilled into your mind through propaganda.

We agreed that the slavery we should be concerned about is the one Bob Marley advised we should free ourselves from- mental slavery. Slavery, we said is what gives life momentum and that before anything can occur in your life, slavery must occur. Before the world manipulators could get that which they wanted from the black race; they had to enslave the mind. Now it is time you realized that propaganda is what gives life to this mental slavery.

It has been said for centuries now that the only thing that you and only you can have control over is your mind. This also means that you are the only one who can think your thoughts, and if man becomes his thoughts and what he thinks he is- then it is only you who can think thoughts that will make you be whatever it is you shall become, and I cannot think thoughts of poverty on your behalf to turn you into a poor being. This can never happen because it is against the laws of creation, for even God first thought about you in his mind before he created you. Can a sculptor create the image of something he cannot see in his mind? Never, he will observe an image and copy, or create from what he sees in his mind. It must start in your mind. You can never own a house for as long as you do not think about it. You must have in your mind thoughts of owning a house before you can ever own one. Before you can join the military, you must first think about joining. You must first harbor military thoughts in your mind before you can finally find yourself serving your nation.

No one has ever become a scientist, who never harbored thoughts of science in his mind; every thief must think about theft in his mind. He first becomes a thief in his mind, through his thoughts and he will see himself as a thief in his mind before we see him steal and get sentenced to jail. It is he who must think the thoughts, not his friends or brothers. It is *as a man thinketh, so he becomes,* and not *"AS YOU THINK FOR A MAN, SO HE BECOMES.*

The thoughts must come from you, and not even your mother can think on your behalf.

"No one else can control your thoughts; even the cruelest tyrant cannot force you to think about something you refuse to accept...the thoughts you allow to dominate your mind will determine what you will get from life." (Napoleon Hill)
If man becomes only what he thinks he is and what he thinks about, and not what someone else thinks he is- and no man can think on your behalf to make you become something; then how can the world manipulators turn the black race into an inferior one, or a poverty-stricken race? The secret is that they will lure you into thinking thoughts that will turn you into a poor man! It is that simple and as fruitful as giving a kid candy and you get to hear the grapevine from the kid.

Therefore, propaganda came into being, to lure you into thinking thoughts as desired by others for life to move as they would like it. If I want you to be a gangster, I will use various means to make you think thoughts of gangster life and how cool it is to be one. I will use the Black Entertainment T.V to entertain you with programs that encourage you to only become entertainers to humanity. I will use the media to show you gangsters making a living, becoming celebrities and millionaires. I will use MTV to showcase former gangsters from your black race, who rose to fame and stardom, minting millions of dollars. You will thereby as a black youth; harbor in your mind thoughts that to become rich- you must start as a gangster. Unfortunately, you are likely to lose your life through the bullet, face jail terms or paralysis, before you rise to stardom.

God used his messengers and prophets to spread his positive propaganda to people, to ensure that man behaves as he willed. Jesus did spread the propaganda of salvation and of the Kingdom of God which was at hand for all humanity. The Apostles' Creed is propaganda to constantly make us think of God as our almighty creator, and Jesus Christ as his only begotten son…, it is positive propaganda that I am proud to instill in my mind daily.

Propaganda is all over, for even the commercials on television and radio is purely propaganda to enslave your mind into buying a certain commodity or service. When people want to be elected to office, they use every possible means to instill propaganda into your minds to lure you to vote for them. When I need a loan from you, I will craft propaganda and instill it in your mind to make you give me the loan. A resume is simply a document of propaganda you will use to sell yourself to the prospective employer, you use it to try and influence his decision on picking the right candidate for the position at hand.

You are dressed and covered in veil purely through propaganda, and the black race can only step out of the veil completely, through propaganda. The devil crafted and delivered his propaganda to Adam and Eve, making them to become slaves to sin. The devil's propaganda to Eve was that contrary to what God told them, they would not die if they ate the fruit in the middle. Instead, they would be "like God and know what is good and what is bad." (Genesis 3:1-5) The two mortals then harbored thoughts of being like God in their minds and the joy that it would give them. They finally ate the fruit, due to the thoughts they thought about. The devil did not think the thoughts on their behalf, but he had to lure them with sweet words that would make them voluntarily think then eat the fruit that was going to give them woes, which was the devil's desire.

Jesus came with the propaganda of salvation to reverse the damage caused by the devil's propaganda; and we are assured of eternal life due to his propaganda of redemption.

Propaganda to reverse the negative effects of the propaganda that led the black race to where it stands today is what we urgently need, but the propaganda must be consistent and long term until the positive desires are achieved and passed to the next generation of youth. Jesus asked his disciples to continue with his propaganda until it was well spread across the four corners of the world- he desired consistency and success in his mission.

The Jews are where they are thanks to the propaganda entailed in the Old Testament of the bible- the torah, which they adhere to, to date. The Arabs are aided by the propaganda of Islam together with the philosophies of life they developed when they landed their hands on the works of the Greeks like Homer and Plato. Asians are known to have had their own positive philosophies which they taught their people and the same is true with the Europeans and the whole white community who owe their civilization to the evident philosophical works of the ancient Greeks and Romans, and not forgetting the stolen works from Egypt. The youths of these races were forced to learn these things written by their poets and philosophers, and we know this to be true for even in the *confessions*, St. Augustine narrates to God how they were forced to learn the works of the poets in the Roman Empire.

The case is different for the entire black race, we only brag about things we claim we did yet we cannot prove. We boast on a large scale about works that do not exist or were stolen from us and are today credited to other races. Instead of spending valuable time and energy arguing that things that have already been connected to the white race are ours, why don't we today create things that have not been tainted and that will with no doubt show us our might? Whatever was stolen from the black race and credited to the whites or Arabs is already strongly imprinted in our minds to glorify them. To reverse this, we must create things that glorify our race. The tainted ones will from time to time take us back into glorifying those other races as we were used to.

Germany was vastly destroyed by the world wars, but Germany today is Europe's largest economy and is highly industrialized and developed. The Germans did not sit down and say- "we were once great", but we were destroyed by our enemies. They said instead that- if they were once great- nothing can stop them from being great again.

Russia is once again becoming a threat to the United States years after the latter broke the Soviet Union. The Russians did not sit down and say- 'we were once the superpowers, but we were destabilized by the Americans'; instead, they told themselves that if they once were- they will again be today, and they started to re-build. So, Africa was once great and we will be great once again, but we must start rebuilding instead of singing about our past greatness.
It all starts in the mind and human beings become only that which they think they are, and what they think about. If we today craft consistent propaganda to make us think and believe that we can become mighty- then as sure as the day follows the night; we will become mighty. But if we continue to think and believe that we were once great and leave it at that, then we will forever remain in the state of "we once were mighty," just as sure as the day will follow the night. Like reggae legend Bob Marley said: *"Get up...stand up for your rights!"*

> *"When someone comes along who can put in words what everyone feels in their hearts, each feels {Yes! That is what I have always wanted and hoped for}"*
>
> *(Joseph Goebbels)*

Chapter Eight

New Social paradigm

It is not enough that we identify the problems we face as a race no matter where we come from in the world. Knowing the enemies of the black race, singling out the causes of our woes, and writing volumes of literature on the same is helpful; but not enough.

A lot has been written since the days when Booker T. Washington wrote *'up from slavery'* in 1901, over a century ago. W.E.B Dubois wrote *'the souls of black folk'* in 1903 and Garvey educated starting in the early nineteen twenties and left us "the history that will inspire the millions that are coming." We even know who the enemy is, we know that we must unite, we know that we must empower ourselves economically, we know that we must have a unified black nation and government in Africa- the Unified Nations in Africa. Question is - what are we still waiting for?

It is time for action and the time is now. We are not about to start a new cause in the struggle for the redemption of the African race. That will be a waste of time for the struggle began centuries ago. My friend Tempestt Little and I happened to be researching on the lives of the Maroons one day, and I was amazed to read that - as early as 1655, the Maroons in Jamaica were already fighting the slave masters and they broke away from the slave camps forming their own communities.

They knew back then that it is paramount that they have a community of their own- independent of the oppressor. Instead of just pleading for their rights and begging to be made equals with the white population, they began forming a community of their own where they were all equal and free men. Why can't we today realize that it is paramount that we have a nation of our own where the various African communities all over the world can call home and live-in full happiness, freedom, and prosperity?

Maroons negotiating peace with colonialists.

Greed, envy, and jealousy are the three plagues that deny us progress. These are the elements entailed in the veil, what the enemy incites us to uphold and practice to ensure that we never prosper. Greed led brothers to sell their own brothers into slavery in Africa, greed led Africans to help the white European powers conquer and colonize them in Africa, whereby they were treated like animals and second-class citizens in their own countries.

Envy and jealousy have for over the centuries ensured that no black movement, no black struggle ever makes the desired progress. Envy, jealousy, and greed have made sure that we have never acted towards solving the problems of our race. The three plagues have made sure that we continuously write and talk about our problems as a race, cry about the solutions- but we never implement any of the solutions we loudly cry for.

Solutions to our problems are already laid down. Competent black thinkers like Marcus Garvey, Booker T. Washington, W.E.B Dubois, Martin Luther King, Malcolm X, Kwame Nkurumah, Julius Nyerere, Prof. Ali Mazrui, Amos Wilson, Bob Marley, Peter Tosh, Burning Spear and many more have put down the road map, and the Burning Spear- Mr. Winston Rodney, actually advised that we should have *"a subject in school on Marcus."* There will never be any new solution, or any better solution to the problems facing the black race but the harmonious amalgamation of the solutions that have already been put before us by the thinkers like the once we mentioned above.

The earlier we come to terms that we already have the solutions and stop wasting time and energy trying to find solutions, then the sooner shall we emancipate our soul. All we need to do is to bring together the works of genius that we already have from the many competent philosophers and think tanks of our race, with great emphasis on the philosophy and opinions of Marcus Garvey.

Jamaican dub poet Mutabaruka advice that:

"African leaders….

Garvey's action we can't duplicate

Black pride him did preach

To the young we must teach

Put Garvey in reality

Make we check him philosophy

Talking about African dignity

In this insanity…"

And as the great Dr. Martin Luther king Jr. said, Garvey "was the first man, on a mass scale level, to give millions of Negroes a sense of dignity and destiny, and make the Negro feel he was somebody" *(Bob Blaisdell; Selected writings and speeches of Marcus Garvey).*

Garvey is the only black man to have left behind a detailed road map to our emancipation and a call to action. He even initiated a correspondence course - *the School of African Philosophy*; aimed at educating black people on their redemption.

Marcus Garvey did not just identify the problems; but he gave us the route to success, and he gathered millions of black people worldwide and began acting- acting towards freeing the black people and taking them home to a unified black nation in Africa, action towards empowering the black race economically with his numerous U.N.I.A business enterprises. Unfortunately, the three plagues caught up with him and we still do not have a unified black nation in Africa, and our race is still enslaved. The enemy used black men to bring Garvey down, together with his emancipation struggle and economical empowering initiatives. It was black men in America who became traitors, betrayers of their own race, same way they were betrayed by members of their own race in Africa at the dawn of slavery.

After careful examination and meditation on the efforts of the various black thinkers and leaders we have today, and those who left their works and memories with us – you will realize that emancipation of the black race will only be achieved successfully when two main projects are created and nurtured. We must create a united socially, politically, and economically powerful black population and unified nations in Africa for all the African communities, where each community is a nation making up the 'The New World Communities' League of Africa' (NWCLA)

Then secondly, we must introduce and spread into the minds of every member of the black race- carefully crafted, positive propaganda that will be beneficial to the race. Propaganda that undoes the harms caused by the negative propaganda instilled by the world manipulators, everything else will fall into place and there will be an abundance of soldiers naturally moving themselves towards their emancipation.

The propaganda will be one that informs you, a member of the black race- on how you can achieve true happiness in life- for that is your goal in life. Life is a pursuit of happiness. It will be Propaganda that shows you who you are, what you can do and what you should do. Peter Tosh said that *"you can't blame the youth,"* if you do not give them the right knowledge and information. Black people, for example-have come to accept that they are second class members of the human race, inferior people who deserve the troubles and discrimination they enjoy. This is what we must change, and it can only be done through propaganda targeted towards the black population.

How many prosperous people do you think we will have due to this positive propaganda? How many scientists do you think we shall have once this is accomplished? How about technological gurus and medical professionals to keep us healthy and cure the biological weapons like AIDS created to exterminate us? How about professional strategists, enlightened intellectuals who are familiar with the black population and their culture- to guide us to heights never seen before, the kind of strategists that the white race and Asians have?

At independence, most countries in Africa like Kenya were economically ahead of most Asian countries like the now industrial giant South Korea. Years down the line, most of those Asian countries are now among the world's industrial, technological, and economic power houses, while the ones in Africa are among the third world beggars and baggers of the world! The Asian countries trained their people, fed them on positive propaganda and eventually gave birth to professional strategists who mapped up the success they enjoy today. Do not expect an outsider to train you to the required heights; you must train yourself to get there. You are the master of your own destiny- we are the masters of the black race's destiny!

It is not the world manipulators who trained the Asians who were at one time below the African nations, training them to become self-dependent, industrialized, and economic giants of the world. The Asians trained themselves, they are training themselves. With the education we have today, all we need now is to train ourselves on the training we lack, which is the propaganda on life- compiled by think tanks of our own race for our race. Propaganda that is tailor made to perfectly suit all our needs as a race. That is what has helped the other races and makes the Arabs think as one just as the Europeans, Jews, Indians, and Chinese think- and that's exactly what's lacking in our black race.

Garvey began on a journey towards the formation of an African Communities' League, and those he influenced like Nkrumah, were for the idea of the creation of a United African Nation, a United States of Africa so to say, a nation in Africa for all black people no matter once current nationality.

Dubois was for the idea of integration in America; blacks to integrate and assimilate into the white population, then progress and prosper ahead in life.

Dr. Martin Luther King, jr had a dream that one day *"little black boys and girls will be able to join hands with little white boys and girls as sisters and brothers."*

Professor Ali Mazrui encourages black people to counter penetrate the western world, mingling with the western communities, making our presence felt and influencing their lifestyles and culture, then gaining from theirs as well.

Prof. Ali Mazrui is also of the view that:

"African unity can only succeed by involving intellectuals" and that it takes "intellectuals and educated minds to conceive and construct an alternative social paradigm,"

A social paradigm that will give us true happiness as human beings, and one that will bridge the gap between the various communities of our race and between our race and the other races of the world.

Incidentally the sage of Tuskegee, Booker T. Washington did start an institute for industrial training of black souls in Alabama. To him, the industrial training and enlightening of the black souls for their economic empowerment; was crucial and of greater relevance than the fight for civil rights. He really was wise back then. How could economically helpless leaders with no training, with no knowledge of self- "conceive and construct an alternative social paradigm" for the freed slaves? Marcus Garvey admired the sage of Tuskegee, and he came to America to raise funds for such an institution in his native Jamaica.

We need an alternative social paradigm and must create a politically and economical powerful and independent unified nations in Africa our motherland.

In the world of today where we have already intermingled and inter married with other races, we cannot create a nation with only blacks as citizens. We have members of our race with parents, siblings, or spouses from different races, and we must take them into consideration. The world is also headed to the creation of one human race as is the will of God, for we are all members of one family which is the family of God. We can create a black nation where every world community is a citizen, a nation with a black government and president, a nation governed by laws written by the black man himself as we had in ancient Egypt; not by laws written by the white supremacists to oppress the black man. Egypt was the first world superpower, the first world 'kingdom' before the Persian, Greek, Roman or even the current American. As it was in the beginning, so shall it be in the end. The ancient black Egypt must first regain its glory before the 'end days.'

As we were in the beginning (in ancient Egypt), so shall we return and this time, as Garvey prophesied; the awakened Africa *"shall never go back to sleep."*

We also need to have positive propaganda fed into the minds of all black people to awaken the soul of this sleeping giant- the true sleeping giant. They tricked us and with the help of the three plagues of our race, together with ignorance - they were able to take our wisdom from Alexandria in Egypt and Timbuktu in Mali; and they used all of it largely for their own benefit while claiming ownership- as they brain washed and held us in mental slavery.

During the early 15th century, the Arabs built the Sankore madrasah known as the University of Sankore in Timbuktu. This was the center from which they spread Islamic and Arabic propaganda to whole of Africa as they converted Africans into Islam. It was a center for the mental slavery of the black population. The three plagues played their designed role as the Africans helped them and even gave away their wisdom in exchange for wealth and power.

We must now spread propaganda that has been *"conceived and constructed by black intellectuals, giving us an alternative social paradigm"* to help achieve our goal. We need to use Institutions for propaganda, same way the Arabs used the University of Timbuktu, and the Greeks used the one we had in Alexandria, Egypt.

We today boast that we once were blah blah, but we have nothing to show of it- while they have everything to show of the wisdom we had.

The time has come for us to do it one more time and show the world that, truly – we were they during the glorious days. This is the time for us to rebuild the pyramids and come up with new fronts in science, astrology, technology, philosophy, and everything that God has blessed us with in order for us to be a blessing to the world. We are now recreating the wisdom they took from Alexandria and Timbuktu, and we shall have everything to show of this wisdom, the world will know for a fact that we were they, the wise and gifted.

Just as they used the University of Timbuktu to enslave our minds, spreading propaganda that only favors them- so shall we use the institutions we will create, to enslave our own minds and spread propaganda that favors our race- the black African race. We shall enslave our minds to the pursuit of true happiness in life for that is the aim in life for every human being as designed by God the creator.

The Movement

Why is it that no serious and genuine black organization has been formed after Garvey's UNIA? A society or organization to implement the realistic thoughts, ideas and hints that have been placed in front of our race since the days when the Maroons formed their own communities, whereby we get the hint that we need to form our own independent community- a Unified Nation in Africa (UNIA) for all Africans' communities. Garvey called it the African Communities' League and he began working towards its formation. We shall therefore look for him in the whirlwind as he prophesied and have him us our guide; for as he said- he was *"but a John the Baptist"* preparing the way for the liberators of our race.

Why is it that we only have black activists and organizations that repeatedly shout about the problems, come up with solutions to the problems of the black African race, but none since Garvey's UNIA has come out to implement the solutions? Making noise on the streets and media is good and it is important, but it is not enough. It is not worth calling 'implementation'.

"Some kind of idea is at the beginning of every political movement. It is not necessary to put this idea in a thick book, nor that it take political form in a hundred long paragraphs...the greatest world movements have always developed when their leaders knew how to unify their followers under short, clear theme" (Joseph Goebbels)

(I am not quoting Mr. Goebbels because he was a good man of exemplary deeds, but because he was and still stands as the best propagandist ever)

What Garvey did is what is called implementation, and he lay down propaganda that suits our race, propaganda tailor made for all our needs. Why do you think that the system is designed to ignore him and his works? Why don't we black people learn the philosophy of Garvey in our learning institutions? The manipulators knew for a fact that Marcus Garvey mapped out the true, concise propaganda and a road map- that if persistently pursued, would have led to our emancipation. Garvey was on a mission not only to form a Unified nation for the Africans, but to free our minds from mental slavery, for even as Martin Luther King Jr. said: Garvey "was the first man, on a mass scale level, to give millions of Negroes a sense of dignity and destiny, and make the Negro feel he was somebody." The manipulators know that the secret of black liberation was revealed in the philosophy and opinions of Marcus Garvey, they therefore manipulated us; and we are still manipulated into not studying our SECRET.

It is time for action, now is the time for action. If not, then we better shut up and stop filling our minds with numerous solutions that we do not intend to implement. If we are not ready to act and change our situation, then let us stop identifying and discussing the problems faced by the black souls. Every time you identify and discuss these problems, you only add salt onto the wound, thereby permanently placing yourself in pain and suffering. You will only be making yourself angrier by repeatedly dwelling on the problems. The only psychological proven method of taking away stress is when you act to solve the cause of the stress. If you dwell on the causes of your stress and keep saying that you are in stress- then you will forever remain stressed.

When you decide to take action and solve the problems we have as a race, you will be bringing an end to the pain and suffering, you'll be healing the wound- you'll be bridging the gap- you'll be receiving reparation for the ills done to you by the slave or colonial masters, you'll be returning and repatriating back to Africa- either physically or mentally whereby your mind will be connected to the parent African soul. Let us now fill our minds with acts and begin at once to solve the problems.

We need a movement. We need to create a society to steer us towards the realization of our emancipation. As sheep, we need a shepherd; we are in jeopardy because we do not have a shepherd. I therefore propose the formation of a society that will propagate a new social paradigm within the black population all over the world. A society that will steer the process of creating the A Unified Nations in Africa (U.N.I.A) for all black folks.

"You can spend ten years giving the antidote to the poison that is produced by a badly led cultural establishment, but a single decree from the Ministry of Culture can destroy all your work. If you had spent that ten years winning fighters for the movement, the movement would have conquered the Ministry of Culture! Everything else is mere piecework...

If a movement wins political power, it can do those positive things it wants to do. Only then does it have the power to protect its accomplishments" (Joseph Goebbels)

**(I am not quoting Mr. Goebbels because he was a good man of exemplary deeds, but because he was and still stands as the best propagandist ever)*

Chapter Nine

The New World Communities' League of Africa (NWCLA)

Government is "a centralized authority for the purpose of expressing the will of the people" (Marcus Garvey). From the U.S declaration of independence, we are informed that "Governments are instituted among Men, deriving their just Powers from the Consent of the Governed."

It is in the Right of the People to alter or abolish .., and to institute a new Government,"

This is a proposal to the formation of a new unified government in Africa, and a new nation. This nation shall be governed by a government that genuinely expresses "the will of the people" of Africa and the entire African race wherever they are in the world.

Since gaining independence from the white colonial masters, African countries have had commendable progress but are still amongst the poorest in the world, dependent on their former colonial masters. The governments are infested by the three plagues of our race which have made sure that there is slow economic growth but a quick growth in the gap between the rich politically correct men and the majority poor citizens.

Tribal fighting, civil wars, poverty, hunger and starvation, corruption in government and institutions, too much suffering is order of the day for most citizens of the nations in Africa. The current governments have failed terribly to express the will of the people in these African nations for we can never believe that the people's will is to have inter-tribal fighting, civil wars, poverty, hunger and starvation, corruption in government and institutions or too much suffering! The people's will is to live happy lives full of joy, liberty and prosperity.

The current governments have for all these decades failed and are unlikely to succeed at solving the problems faced by the Africans in the continent because they were never at conception "instituted among Men, deriving their just Powers from the Consent of the Governed." Neither were they created to wholly express "the will of the people" of Africa, but that of the veil, the will of the world manipulators.

What is happening in Africa today is what the world manipulators willed when they created and instituted the current governments in Africa. The yoke of colonialism in Africa, as Jaramogi Oginga Odinga said was simply passed on to the Africans by the European powers.

"Question arose whether real decolonization was winning formal independence or the collapse of the colonial state instead. Is decolonization comprised of changing of the guards on Independence Day, raising the new flag and singing the new national anthem, while leaving the old structures intact? Is it the cruel and bloody disintegration of colonial structures?" *(Prof Ali Mazrui, East African Standard, 10th Feb 2008)*

The East African Standard recently published an interesting revelation on September 20th, 2008, with regards to Jomo Kenyatta who was the founding president of Kenya. The information in this revelation is not unique to Kenya but was the norm for most of the African countries receiving independence only different tactics and baits were used and it did not have to be land.

The newspaper article was entitled **"Secret land deal that made Kenyatta first president"** and it revealed how Kenyatta "entered a secret pact with the British government not to interfere with the skewed land distribution at independence. In return, the British would clear his way as independent Kenya's first leader." According to a memo written to the then governor representing the Queen of England in Kenya (Malcolm MacDonald), by the then leader of the white settlers in the country (Sir Michael Blundell) – the British *"handpicked Kenyatta to be Kenya's first president"* and was given conditions and told that he'll only become president "but only if he could personally give assurance that **he had abandoned the extremist anti-white views he held!!!"**

At independence, Kenyans rejoiced, thinking that they had a president who represented their will, one of their own. Little did they know that he was representing their will only in veil while representing the British will out of the veil. One is left praying for the day a South African newspaper will publish revelations of some kind, concerning any secret pact that might have been signed with any of the leaders in South Africa to enable the whites to continue dominating in the country.

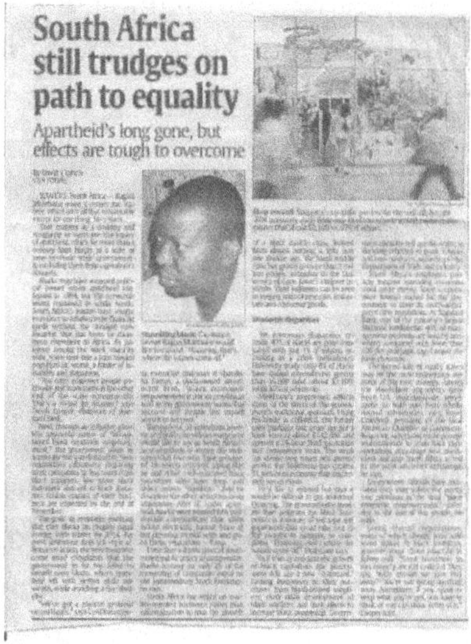

Newspaper cutting from USA Today.

In the above newspaper cutting from USA today, we read that:

"Blacks (in South Africa) may have assumed political power when apartheid collapsed in 1994, but the economic levers remained in white hands. " In this news article written by David Lynch, we are also informed that: *"the government so far (South African government) has failed to benefit most blacks whom apartheid left with neither skills nor wealth, while enriching a tiny black elite."*

These black elite are the ones infested by the plagues, those who represent our will in veil- the ones we today rely on to lead us to the 'Promised Land'. Will they ever lead us there? Maybe in veil!

The veil recently turned South Africans wild and sent them killing and evicting away from their country - their brothers and sisters from other African countries. This they did without realizing that the real enemy, the one responsible for their dwelling in the shanties of Soweto, was the same one they had been fighting against for years, who then gave them independence in veil. Incidentally, it is the same bunch of enemies that gave Kenya a president through the veil, and so were other African countries.

The governments in Africa are but in veil, covered in veil- making us see the world manipulators as our redeemers. We are still under colonization, but the veil makes us see freedom, liberty and equality. The veil makes us see as though we are governing ourselves, we see black leaders in our governments in Africa but when you step out of the veil you see the white supremacists to be our governments. Our governance is a puppet show, it is a marionette entertainment, and the world manipulators pull the strings to their own tunes and pleasure. In the Kiswahili book *mashetani*, it was called 'ukoloni mambo leo'- (neo- colonialsm).

Mashetani is Kiswahili for ghosts, or spirits. The real rulers of Africa are unseen- they are like ghosts. The people we see are just puppets of the ghosts. Africa is led by some spirit that has possessed the

African people to dance to its tune. When we demanded independence from the white settlers, all they did was give it to us in veil. They then changed form and become ghosts and now colonize us in invisible form and as usual, they use and lure our own (leaders) to harm us.

Jaramogi Oginga Odinga, the pioneer of multi-party democracy in Kenya; gave us the hint that we still do not have independence in Africa as was the title of his book *'not yet uhuru'* – *not yet independent/ free*. Africa is still under the colonial masters and only free in the veil. It is only free in veil, and we also never freed our colonized minds, yet the veil resides in the mind! And it was the mind that was first colonized, which means that it should have been the first one to be freed- "emancipate yourselves from mental slavery."

Stepping out of the veil I see the three plagues attacking our leaders and governments in Africa, same way the Africans were attacked when they sold their brothers into slavery, same way they helped the Europeans to colonize them in their own homeland in Africa. Only the game has changed, for it is dressed in veil, a veil that can only be ripped off when the Africans' minds receive the propaganda that will awaken life in the souls of these intelligent people.

All over Africa there is a cry for change and independence, The Africans in the continent want no more pain and suffering for God did not create us for that. Tribal fighting, civil wars, poverty, hunger and starvation, corruption in government and institutions, too much suffering is all we have received from the current governments- it is time for change- time to form a new government in Africa that truly represents the will of the people, nobody in Africa willed to have pain and suffering, how can we desire suffering? We desire happiness and the current governments do not represent that.

I do hereby strongly support the formation of a united African government that truly represents and addresses the will of the people of Africa. We cannot trust, nor rely on the current leaders or governments, who are dressed in veil to steer us towards a government that is living out of the veil. We should therefore have a shepherd who is out of the veil tearing the veil from the hearts, souls, and minds of every African.

The current governments and leaders have been attacked by the deadly communicable plagues- and we will be endangering ourselves further if we rely on them. The African Union is a union of the plagues, a union in veil. How can leaders who have failed to lead their countries into prosperity claim to come together to lead a whole continent into prosperity? Are they not the same people promoting dictatorship, poor governance and lots of pain and sufferings in their countries?

Ethnicity is creating a huge gap between the various communities in Africa. This is a serious hindrance towards African unity which is paramount to the salvation of our race, for how can we bridge the gap between Africans in the motherland and those abroad, when those in the motherland are disunited? How do we expect to attract siblings back to their home when their fellow siblings wrangle and kill each other back at home?

Africa is underdeveloped, Running, piped tap water is unavailable in majority of households in Africa, how will the African American move away from the lifestyle suitable for this century, to one where former British Prime minister- Tony Blair, once compared its conditions to those in Europe during the years Before Christ (BC)? Let's be realistic, how can you migrate from a developed land, a world superpower- into a land that is the laughing image to the world, where poverty is considered 'normal' way of life and charity is what the people pray for everyday? The citizens of Africa are every day becoming more charity expectant, than economic development expectant.

We must first unify the Africans in the motherland and form a powerful unified government there. A government that will establish rapid growth and prosperity to reverse the current stagnation in growth and prosperity that has seen the Asian nations overtake the African nations that were way ahead of them during their independence.

Africa must first become a political and economic powerhouse before we can bridge the gap among the various African communities scattered all over the world

Fulfillments

Dubois was for assimilation; well, we shall assimilate with members of the white race as he preached – but in our own country in Africa, same way we did assimilate with other races in ancient Egypt.

We shall equally assimilate the western technology and advancements and create better technology. We shall assimilate every God loving world religion; assimilate everything good- anything that does not put man distances away from his creator shall be assimilated in our New World Communities' League in Africa.

Martin Luther King Jr's dream will not come true because Obama is the U.S president. "Little black boys and girls" are not guaranteed that they'll "be able to join hands with little white boys and girls as sisters and brothers," simply because there is or there once was a black president of The United States of America.

The dream will not fully come true before Garvey's preaching of self-reliance for black people is realized. Now you understand why the sage of Tuskegee gave industrial training and acquisition of wealth by the black population top priority as opposed to the fight for equality? How can you demand equality from a man you are dependent on? From a man you beg from. In human reality, you are not equal and are demanding for what you do not deserve. He may treat you as an equal only as a public relations ploy, but in his mind, you are inferior, and his actions will show you that he doesn't genuinely see you to be his equal.

When we empower ourselves socially and economically; then build our powerful nation in Africa, MLK's dream will come true in the minds of humanity for only then can it come true in the physical. So do not be deceived by the veil today that the struggle is over because Americans elected the first African American president.

Prof. Ali Mazrui encourages that "counter penetrating the west" is vital towards bridging the gap between us and the world; we shall now counter penetrate the west in Africa- in the NWCLA. We have for hundreds of years counter penetrated abroad, it is now time to utilize the loot in terms of exposure, knowledge and enlightenment that we have gained from this counter penetration since the days of slavery and colonialism.

Even as the Greeks and Romans used to take home the spoils after conquering the enemies, so shall we now take home the vast loot from the west. The Greeks counter penetrated us in ancient Egypt at Alexandria and gained a lot in terms of exposure and knowledge. This they took back home to develop their civilization, wisdom, and the works we adore and use today. Plato the brilliant Greek philosopher travelled, and counter penetrated the world up to Egypt, he took his gains back home and formed the famous academy where he shared the spoils with his countrymen- spreading knowledge to his people-feeding them with the positive propaganda necessary to make them better people. Why can't we also take home the spoils we have gained from the west so far and form academies where we shall share the spoils with our country men- spreading knowledge to our people- feeding them with the positive propaganda necessary to make them better people?

By so doing, we shall create a new outstanding civilization then the world will be the ones seeking us. It will be the world yearning to counter penetrate the Africans in their nations in the NWCLA, same way they did in ancient Egypt. As it was in the beginning, so shall it be again…in the end.

"Politics is governed not by moral principles, but by power."

(Joseph Goebbels)

(I am not quoting Mr. Goebbels because he was a good man of exemplary deeds, but because he was and still stands as the best propagandist ever)

"So here we stand among thoughts of human unity, even though conquest and slavery; the inferiority of black men, even if forced by fraud; a shriek in the night for the freedom of men who themselves are not yet sure of their right to demand it. This is the tangle of thought and afterthought wherein we are called to solve the problem of training men for life" *(W.E.B Dubois, The souls of Black Folk)*

Chapter Ten

<u>Specialized Institutions of Learning</u>

Knowledge is strength, information is power, and education is the key to success in life. Don't you, as a member of the black race desire success in life? Desire strength and power to enable you to be successful in whatever you want, and to be able to protect your success? Who does not want success in life? Every human being, every member of the black race is living life in pursuit of happiness, which is brought about through success; success in the things that you embark on with an aim of achieving certain goals that will lead to your being happy.

Education that truly opens the doors to success in your life is what we lack as black people all over the world. Knowledge and information that truly gives us strength and power, is what we lack as black people all over the world. If we had all these we would not today be as inferior and the least successful group in the world.

To truly help the black race, you must start by acknowledging the inferiority we dwell in and the fact that we are the least successful group in the world today as a race, though we have brains and potential like no other race in the same world. No need of being ashamed or alarmed for we now know why we are the way we are, and due to this knowledge, we can now reverse the situation and become the most successful group in the world as a race, and this is why we began the book by stating the importance of knowing and accepting the truth even if it hurts. The truth is always the redeemer.

The knowledge, information, and education that we have been receiving has been in veil and its fruits can be seen when you look at the lives and conditions of the black race, be it as an African American, an African in the Caribbean, Europe or in the mother land.

We have too much a numerous population of educated black people but not an equally numerous population of successful black people in the world. How can this be the case when education is the key to success? The education possessed by the black people is in veil. We need true education that leads to success, education that will also *"furnish the black world with adequate standards of human culture and lofty ideals of life."* (W.E.B Dubois: The souls of black folk)

We need people who are *"broad minded, and cultured... to scatter civilization among people (the black race) whose ignorance was (is) not simply of letters, but of life itself."* (W.E.B Dubois)

Stepping out of the veil, I hereby propose the formation of Institutions of science, research and learning that will avail to the entire black population all over the world the true knowledge that gives strength, the true Information that gives them power and true education that ensures they become successful in life. Stepping out of the veil, you will ask yourself how you came to believe that the enemy would give you knowledge that would give you the mental strength required if you are to see out of the veil and challenge him, strength that would allow you to live outside of the veil. You will ask yourself why you believed that the enemy would give you information that would give you the power to reject his authority over you in a world where we are all created equal by God and no man has a right to rule and oppress the other; a world where *"no one human being has any more power than any other,"* as described by Robert Collier in his book *the secret of the ages*.

We must prepare veils that will suit our needs, and begin to wear them immediately, for us to reverse the negativity brought to all black people by the veils prepared and given to us by the world manipulators. It has always been the veil and we shall free ourselves only through the veil.

Success leads to independence and independent people are not slaves who do as someone else pleases. Stepping out of the veil, you will ask yourself how you believed that the enemy was feeding you with the education that is the key to success in life.

The Greeks educated themselves, the Romans did the same, and so did the Arabs and Asians. Why can't we do the same? They formed unifying philosophies and taught their people on the same. They structured their education and delivered it to their people to make them successful in life. Why can't we structure our education, and tailor make it to perfectly conform to our standards and needs? The white man is not seen to be inferior in the world; he therefore has no time preparing a syllabus to correct inferiority in a race. By relying entirely on his education, we will never have the education that corrects inferiority complex in our race.

"Nobody can give you freedom. Nobody can give you equality or justice or anything. If you are a man, you take it" (Malcom X)

I do not propose the mere formation of black owned institutions, but the education of African philosophy and concepts. Education that will produce numerous black intellectuals to dilute the numerous numbers of entertainers who enrich the white controlled media and help spread propaganda that encourages the black youth to only dream of being entertainers, whilst portraying the negative side of the hip hop and bling culture, complete with the sagging of pants, and driving of fancy cars as the most desirable traits in life.

The enemy uses the media to show his intellectual might and to impress in our minds that he is superior, while through the hip hop culture, blacks are lured by the media to believe that we are only good at entertaining and use of foul language and that we can be relied upon to entertain to the world's satisfaction. It makes us proud of getting locked up in the prisons and we glorify and praise those who began successful music carriers after getting locked up in prison. This culture negatively makes the youth grow up believing that life is all about sex, drugs, and money, calling women *bitches** and treating them like animals, making girls pregnant then dumping them, driving fancy cars, buying unnecessarily huge gold chains instead of investing your money and time in some education. Can we blame the youth? We can't, for as long as the black community condones it, and hip-hop music and culture promotes it. Remember Peter Tosh: ***"you can't blame the youth"***. We must blame the black churches, leaders, schools and teachers, parents, the whole black community, and more so the media (B.E.T inclusive). The youth grow up to do what they are taught and what they see, including what they see on B.E.T or on the black music videos, black comedy shows and black movies on T.V

We do not just need black owned institutions for the sake of being black owned. We would rather have white owned institutions that promote a new social paradigm, where black people impress to the world that they are equally superior and show the intellectual might possessed by the race. Institutions that train teachers who will in turn teach the black youth the true desirable traits of life, the desirable possessions of life- the meaning of life.

Higher learning Institutions where we shall initiate positive propaganda that reverses the negative one that exists in our minds today; institutions to create a new social paradigm for the black race.

Part Two

(Anti Hypnosis Poetry)

1. <u>Mystery is the Africans history</u>

Black people a mystique

Black race a mystery

Black race divine mystery

If mystery

Then unknown.

If divine

Then only the High knows

Black history erase

Black history alter

Black history you can suppress

But

Black history

Is in the

Black mystery

If a mystery and unknown

How can you erase or alter

How do you erase or alter what you don't know?

Only the High can erase or alter

They try to erase and alter

But the mystery is the history

Mystery is the black race

Divine is the mystery.

Chapter Two

2. <u>Mystery of the Africans history</u>

Black is mystique

Black people a mystery

Black people mystery

Is in the

Black people history

Black people history

Is not

Black people mystery

Black people mystery

Black Divine mystery

Black people mystery

Is in the

Black people history

Because the

Mystery is the history.

<u>Chapter Three</u>

3<u>. Ashamed of being Ashamed of my being black</u>

Yes I am

I am black

An African I am.

Dark my skin, black my color

I am black

Black man story

Black my complexion

Complex my story

Black as tar my color

True symbol of African

Black my symbol, yet

Black isn't my future.

Black is not the symbol-

Of the black man future

You are black- you are an African

Whoever, wherever, whenever

Yes I am

I am

I am who

I am who I am

Black man I am

African my family

Human my race

Black my story

This is black man story-

Black to be happy

Because

Dark I am dark

But dark is not my future

Yes I am

Complex my story

This is my complex story-

Ashamed I am not

Dark man story

This is dark man story-

African they made a shame;

Black they shamed

Shaming shame

Is the symbol of our future

Shame on shame

Because

I am ashamed of being ashamed.

Yes I am

I am proud to be ashamed;

To be ashamed of ever being ashamed to be black

Because

I am ashamed of ever being ashamed of my being black

Because

Dark I am dark

But dark is not my future

Black they shamed

African they made a shame

Shame we shame

Shame we make a shame

Because bright is our future

Are you ashamed?

Ashamed enough, that you'll never be ashamed?

Will you ever be ashamed that you are black?

I am proud

That I will never be ashamed

Yes I am

I am black

An African I am

<u>Chapter Four</u>

4. <u>Anti-Hypnosis (Anti Blackipulation)</u>

It was said then,

Even as it is said now-

By them who said it not then

But say it now.

They say it today,

Because it was said then.

Those who said it then,

Those still living

Still say it now.

They who say it now-

Say it like it was said then,

Like it is said every day.

It was said then,

Even as it is called today,

Dark it was called then

As it is called now, even by them-

Who know not why 'dark' it's called.

But since it was said then

They have to say it now

 As it is called now – 'dark',

Darker than then

When bright they 'darkened'

It was called 'dark,'

As bright as it was.

It was said then

Even as it is darkened now,

By them who darkened it then.

Children of them who -

Darkened it then, darken it now.

Worse; they darken place today.

Place full of light,

But people see darkness.

Bright in ancient Egypt

Rumored dark today.

Their minds were darkened

As they were hypnotized.

It was said then

Even as they are hypnotized today,

They were hypnotized then.

Darkness they see, yet

Bright is their future

As it was bright then

When their brains

Were darkened;

As their brightness

Is darkened today.

But place can not be darkened

As it is not dark today.

It was said then

But it is said today,

Place is not 'dark'

As it has never been

As it can never be,

Only the minds were darkened,

Enlighten the minds and -

Alas! Place is bright

As bright as our brains,

As it was bright then

As I brighten it today

As we brighten it together.

It was said then

But we stop them now

As we revolutionize our thinking,

As we see the light

That we were told was 'dark.'

Place is wealthy, but wealth is darkened –

and is stolen, as was stolen

When they stole away citizens

Away from place

Enslaved and brutalized them

Colonized and dehumanized-

Those left behind.

Chapter Five

5. <u>The Mwafrika's Creed</u>

I am an African of the African race which is also the black race.

I was created by the one living God,

   Almighty creator of heaven and earth,

The same God who created members

   of every other race in the world.

He created members of every race equally, and with equal abilities.

God created me in his own image and in his likeness,

   just as he did to those of the other races

And what they can do, I can also do- and sometimes even better!

I am black, and I know that for as long as I am black-

   I am an African

My nationality doesn't matter

   because as a member of the black race,

My real nationality is determined not by my country of birth

   or citizenship.

My real nationality as a black person-

   is determined by my being black

My identity and real nationality is African

I am proud to be an African

I will never be ashamed because I am an African

My future as an African is bright

   because God promised and blessed us.

I believe that whoever God bless, no man can curse.

Africa my motherland is blessed by God. It is wealthy,

It's beautiful and I desire to live there

I support the unification of all African people

from all over the world.

I believe that 'nationhood is the strongest security of any race'

 I support the creation of a Unified Nations In Africa -

   for all black people

My duty and mission as an African,

Is to contribute in the motivation and awakening

of the sleeping consciousness of my people,

I should encourage every member of the African race

to desire for Africans all over the world to come together

Epilogue

The mission

Our mission is to arouse the sleeping consciousness of the members of the African race everywhere in the world, to the point where every member of the race will, as one consented body- act for his and her own preservation, preservation of his and her race, and for the good of all humanity. We shall work towards the glorious realization of an emancipated race and a constructed, competent nation for the black race in Africa. Nationhood is the strongest security of any people, and it is for that which we shall strive.

"Be as proud of your race today as our fathers were in the days of yore. We have a beautiful history, and we shall create another in the future that will astonish the world.

All of us may not live to see the higher accomplishment of an African empire- so strong and powerful, as to compel the respect of mankind, but we in our lifetime can so work and act as to make the dream a possibility within another generation…

A race without authority and power is a race without respect…, to free Africa; we must first free ourselves mentally, spiritually, and politically.

Marcus Garvey

<u>**Appreciation**</u>

This is to congratulate the African sages of yesteryears and those of today whose works and thoughts were aimed at the redemption of our race. This is for all the men and women who dedicated their lives to the bettering of the Africans, either at home or abroad. They might have been successful in their mission, may have been unsuccessful, or might have erred; but they played a most crucial role in this struggle and for that reason, I honor them by writing this book.

Reading this book out of the veil, you notice the amalgamation of thoughts and ideas that have been passed on to us from our past sages up to those of today. Amongst them, there are those who I may not agree with all their ideas completely, but a percentage of their thoughts are helpful to our race today, and that is what's important to the black race.

Africans had an oral tradition, whereby information was passed on from one generation to the other through stories told to the young ones, who were the future of the various African communities. Children would gather around their grandparents, who would then pass on information to them, about their traditions, history, and culture. It seems that what lacked was a situation whereby the children were given information that made them love members of their race, or that glorified their race. Not even information that showed them that it was heroic to protect your race from any harm. Looks like they were never told stories that would make them want to better their race, otherwise, this information would have been passed down to us- the generation of today, as was the African tradition. The black race would have been prosperous and united.

The Pan-Africanist Manifesto is an amalgamation of crucial thoughts from various thinkers of the African race, both at home and abroad. In Kenya, we have a spirit of togetherness called *Harambee*. It simply means to bring together, putting our efforts together for the betterment of the community. This book is some harambee, it is a harambee of thoughts and ideas put together, with an aim of uplifting the African race. It will inspire the generation of today, presenting to them in one volume, a collection of intelligent proposed ways which if implemented; will see all black people FREE! Free from mental slavery, for that is the problem of humanity today.

If today's generation fails, which is likely to be the case; then this book will act like the grandparents in the African oral tradition. It will present to the future generation, what their sages said that they need to do, to liberate themselves from the shackles and woes that the past generations voluntarily went through. The black generation of today has been severely brain washed that the future of our race is entirely dependent on the youth, who are the future of our race.

Our race still stagnates, even as other races prosper, because we do not put into implementation our philosophies on life. We instead keep trying to come up with more philosophies, whereas the philosophy needed to uplift our race already exists, though scattered all over. Love is the greatest commandment, and for the love of my race; I hereby present to it 'many things which if read with patience, will show how a race shall be redeemed'. This is to inspire and guide the race towards action, but not towards coming up with more theories. This book is not for theoretical purposes, but a practical guide for the uplifting of the black race as was intended by the sages who inspired it, like Booker T. Washington, Malcom X, Martin Luther King jr, Kwame Nkurumah, Jaramogi Oginga Odinga, Prof. Ali Mazrui, Julius Nyerere, Bob Marley, Peter Tosh, Burning Spear and the entire Rastafarian community, and of course the numerous who I haven't mentioned since the number is too numerous.

It is easy to notice that two forces were of most influence in the writing of this book. Surprisingly, these two forces were in some sort of conflict when they were being propagated, yet these two forces are of the utmost relevance to the black man story. One was more intellectual, in my view intended to stimulate the black leaders to think and come up with solutions needed to better our race, while the other was more for the populace- inspiring action and implementation of the solutions needed to better the black population. It is for this reason, that the forces of W.E.B Dubois and Marcus Garvey dominate this book.

For Garvey's dominant influence in the writing of this book, I will remind you that Garvey promised the enemy that before he goes, he "shall have laid a foundation for other Garveys who will be more deadly in their sting than the one who passes off" He also promised the enemy that "if the enemy could only know that Marcus Garvey is but a John the Baptist in the wilderness" clearing the way ahead of the liberators of Africa.

To the African people, both at home and abroad, I wish to say that I write, not to do away with the teachings of our sages, but to strengthen them for the unification of the African people both at home and abroad, and the freeing of the soul of black people which is enslaved, only to be set free when *Africa will be a blessing to the entire world.*". Israel was God's chosen land, and the Israelites were his chosen people, but Africa is God's Promised land to the entire world today, and The Africans are God's chosen people to be a blessing to the entire world.

Augustine J. Jeffrey

Easter 2010

Facebook: @TheArtofWorldlyLiving

Email: augustinejjeffrey@gmail.com